IMAGES OF JUSTICE

TREVOR GORING

Vol. 1

WOMEN IN-LAW

Second edition
limited to 950 copies
handbound, numbered and signed by the artist.

613/950 ....

....

Published in 1996 by JustArt International.
C8, 202 St-Zotique West, Montreal,
Quebec, Canada, H2V 4S9

ISBN 0-9681407-0-X

To the memory of
my in-laws
Nina and John Richmond.

ACKNOWLEDGMENTS

I take this opportunity
to thank friends, family and colleagues
who have been of immeasurable help in the
production of this first volume. Special thanks
to Professor Jon Breslaw and to Steve Luxton for
his editing and generous help with the text.
I should also like to express
my appreciation to those who have
assisted over the years in bringing my
"Images of Justice"
to the legal community and above all to pay tribute
to my collectors, whose belief in, and commitment to
my art has made it all possible.

PREFACE

The title *Women In-Law* brings to mind two highly disparate images. A major vehicule for the disparagement of women has been the image of the ugly, hostile, malicious mother -in-law. Against this we can set the creative, strong, peace promoting images of Trevor Goring's *Women In-Law.*

Until very recently law has been almost entirely the domain of men. But late twentieth century law schools have experienced a revolution in this regard: fifty percent of entering students are now women. Gender inequality in the leadership of the legal profession persists however and to remedy this situation a great deal still needs to be done. This work will be easier if we, as women in law, can find a deep heritage that supports us in our desire to contribute to the law and our dreams and visions for it.

Memory is "one way of knowing" and the millenia of history that we see in the women in law from antiquity, portrayed in this book, connects us with that memory. Recently, there has been a much greater consciousness in our society of the extent to which we have come to rely solely on reason as the basis of our decision making. We need to add "other ways of knowing" to reason. These include, as well as memory, common sense, moral intuition, creativity and in particular, ethics. One task of women in law will be to integrate, in a responsible way, these "other ways of knowing" into our legal systems.

It is sometimes said that relationships between intimates are governed by morality or ethics, and those between strangers by law. In our post-modern world, it is increasingly difficult to draw clear lines between when one is dealing with an intimate or with a stranger. This means that one of the twenty-first century challenges for law will be to create a legal framework that will allow the integration of law and ethics. Women in law are likely to take a leadership role in constructing this framework.

In the archetypal image of *Iusticia* holding the scales of justice and the sword of mercy we can find a symbolic integration of the male and female, the ethical and the legal, the reasoned and the intuitive. *Mercy* is traditionally regarded as an attribute of women, *Justice* as an attribute of men. And yet, the symbol for mercy is the male, phallic one of the sword and that for justice the balanced symbol that evokes the image of the female breasts. One can muse that our ancient sisters-in-law knew of the need for integration to achieve the wise, humane, ethical application of law, which is essential to the formation, maintenance and protection of human community.

Our challenge in the twenty-first century is to convert our global society to a global community. Meeting Trevor Goring's *Women In-Law,* who faced equally demanding tasks in their eras, will give us courage, hope, a sense of humour in the sense of balance, and some ancient wisdom.

Margaret A. Somerville, AM, FRSC, LL.D.
Gale Professor of Law
McGill University, Montreal

CONTENTS

INTRODUCTION

The law is central to human experience. It is a reflection of the everyday practices of society which yet expresses some of humanity's highest ideals. Embracing all human emotion - often in a most dramatic and theatrical fashion- it is the receptacle of ethical, moral, and practical issues, dealing with discord and concord, innocence and guilt, punishment and reward.

Can it be of any wonder then that the very beginnings of the profession reach back to earliest mythology and share common attributes throughout the world's great cultures? What may, however, come as a surprise is that the very sources of justice, the wellsprings of equity, fairness, peace and protection are indisputably from the feminine realms. Yet, does not justice nurture us, like a mother who nurtures her young? Doesn't she guide our behaviour so that we might keep chaos at bay and continue to civilize ourselves and each other?

For myself, I can't forget the penetrating stare of Wisdom and Justice in the town hall of Siena, Italy. Conscience stands high and well above a wealth of 18th century French iconology. Maat,the Egyptian Goddess, keeps constant watch as I practice my art. In fact, we are all inexorably bound to a marvellous family of women who enhance our lives with their historical truths and with the steady light of justice.

Many, but not all these significant female figures are gathered here, and I hope that later editions will include, among others, the illusive Syn, Scandinavian Goddess who presides at trials as defender against perjurious testimony; and also the sacred courtesan Ishtar, whom the Babylonian scriptures called Righteous Judge, Framer of all Decrees. But the nucleus of the family is with us; through these pages may they speak to you as one.

For though we have met the law and know it to be us, now we have met justice and know it to be she.

ALL'S LOVE, YET ALL'S LAW.

the plates

MAAT

MAAT

*Lady of heaven, Queen of the earth, Mistress of the underworld,** her trinity rules all three realms.

Maat, the Egyptian Goddess, personifies truth and justice, equity and ethics. Her particular symbol is the elegant white ostrich feather, a hieroglyph of truth that always graces her headdress. The Gods themselves are constrained to live by "Maat" and as Chief Justice she is always present, with her male consort, Toth, at the weighing of the heart of the deceased.

Lawgiver of archaic Egypt her "goodness to the suffering" and exercise of "justice with no trace of vengeance" made for notably benevolent laws compared to the stern edicts of later patriarchal Gods. Her feather of truth remains today in legal, ceremonial regalia and is a symbol shared by North American Native tribes.

Painting her in a modern manner, as a contemporary, is to affirm her lasting power in the Pantheon of the law....

*Italics denote quotations. See "Notes on the Texts" for sources.

Great is Maat, the mighty and unalterable!

THEMIS

THEMIS

In Olympus Themis reigns as Divine Justice and Chief Assessor of all humanity. The rights of hospitality lie under her protection. Called "Soteira" by the people, she tirelessly defends the homeless and oppressed. Her parents are the Greek deities Uranus and Gaea, and by Zeus, she is the mother of the Horae (seasons) and Morae (fates) who enforce her jurisdiction.

Rare are Themis' appearances in art history but in each, her presence and demeanor are striking. She is the brilliant charioteer on the north frieze of the Siphnian Treasury at Delphi. She proffers a bay branch and phial in a red-figured cup from 5th century B.C. In the work of an Eleusinian painter 340 B.C., Themis displays remarkable informality and ease of physical stance, made possible by her absolute control of the Delphic Oracle.

In my painting she is portrayed holding the staff of justice, denoting authority and protection. The brimming cornucopia symbolizes her blessing of bountiful order and hospitality.

SOTEIRA *the Saving Goddess*

WISDOM & JUSTICE

WISDOM & JUSTICE

Justice without wisdom is impossible for wisdom concerns itself with the ultimate nature of things and the ultimate good for humanity. *Justice is the lawful and the fair.*

From one of the finest frescoes of Mediaeval Europe comes this powerful allegorical rendition of good civil government and peace. Suspended gracefully in the heavens is the winged figure of Wisdom, "Sapientia". In one hand she holds the scriptures, or Book of Wisdom; in the other, huge gold scales balanced by the enthroned figure of Justice below.

My painting reflects the style of late Mediaeval realism, with its lingering penchant for abstraction and early Renaissance fascination with the visible world. The implicit coda is, "Love justice you who govern the world."

The gift of wisdom sustains the task of justice.

The gift of wisdom sustains the task of justice.

THREE SISTERS

THREE SISTERS

I sought my soul, but my soul I could not see. I sought my Gods, but my Gods eluded me. I sought my sisters, and I found all three.

Three civic sisters from 14th century Italy, three sisters of civil law each with their unique character and allegorical story to tell.... Two are from Florence: the first, headscarf flowing, bears a book of law and scales, while the second wields the traditional sword, most untraditionally as fulcrum, with the globe or affairs of the world balanced against the piercing hook of trade and commerce. From Siena comes the third sister. With sword of strength and crown of just rewards in hand, she sets herself to the defense of the law.

Sometimes you may hear their three eloquent voices in unison: *Seek the good, avoid evil. Do good to others, injure no-one and render to all their own.* I listen closely for them: *for there is no friend like a sister, in calm or stormy weather.*

She is a bowl of golden water which brims
but never overflows

She is both your mirror and your opposite

She is both your mirror and your opposite

She stands between one

and life's cruel circumstances

IVSTI TIA

IUSTICIA

IUSTICIA

Iusticia guards, nourishes and rewards those who treasure her, for she is *the constant and perpetual wish to render to everyone their due.* Pythagoreans taught that "iusticia" and "aequitas" (justice and equity) are *innate attributes of the feminine nature principle.* The Roman Praetor or judge gave expression to justice as the voice of Bona Dea-Fauna-Fatua or the "feminine godhead."

Raphael, the foremost painter of his time, was commissioned in 1510 by Pope Julius II to transform the chamber in the Vatican where legal briefs were signed. His vast ceiling composition encompasses the world in four medallions containing allegorical figures of Theology, Jurisprudence, (Iusticia) Philosophy and Poetry - four symbolic representations of beleaguered humanity's striving toward higher civilization.

My image of Iusticia shows her simply, traditional sword and scales in hand. Elegantly poised, she is *the shield of innocence, the guard of truth... The gladsome light of jurisprudence....*

Justice, like the bright sun,
shall break majestic forth

Justice, like the bright sun,
shall break majestic forth

PORTIA

PORTIA

The quality of mercy is not strained, it droppeth as the gentle rain from heaven, upon the place beneath: It is twice blessed; it blesseth him that gives and him that takes.

The ties of love and friendship unite humankind where justice merely governs interaction. What men and women do for one another from the generosity of love far exceeds the commands of justice. That is why mercy and charity are called to qualify justice, or even set it aside.

In this painting, Portia clearly insists on the letter of the law, while subtly inspiring us to bethink the quality of mercy. For *mercy among the virtues is like the moon among the stars. It is the light that hovers above the judgment seat.*

Earthly power doth then show likest God's,
when mercy seasons justice

Earthly power doth then show likest God's,
when mercy seasons justice

CONSCIENCE

CONSCIENCE

Conscience, or "knowing together," is a word coined by Stoic philosophers to embody divine presence in the human mind. It developed out of Oriental teachings regarding the fusion of man with God, woman with Goddess.

My painting is of one of the most remarkable images of a woman from the Iconologia, or handbooks of personifications used by journeymen sculptors and engravers throughout the 17th and 18th centuries. Crammed with pictoral motifs depicting La Condition Humaine, these are compendiums of potent, deep-seated allegory.

For all of us, Conscience walks a narrow track bordered by flowers and thorns, between the way of an all-too- easy moral sense and the difficult route of *a peace above all earthly dignities, a still and quiet conscience.* As she walks, she attentively considers in her mirror *that little spark of celestial fire in her breast*: *conscience.*

Even when there is no law,

there is conscience

Even when there is no law,

there is conscience

NOTES ON THE PLATES

All colour plates are reproductions of original paintings in the series "Images of Justice". Executed on paper in acrylic, ink and graphite, these originals were inspired by the rich historical tapestry of legal iconography and draw specifically on the following sources.

MAAT

After an upper fragment of a bas-relief from the tomb of Seti I, 19th dynasty, Egypt, c1306-1290 B.C. Original painting, 1994, private collection, Michael Colley, Columbus, Ohio.

THEMIS

After a fresco from Pergamon, c 150 B.C., from the Basilica at Herculaneum. Museo Nazionale, Naples. Original painting, 1995, private collection, Diane Hallatt, Sheffield, U.K.

WISDOM & JUSTICE

After a fragment of the fresco, "The Virtues of Good Government," by Ambrogio Lorenzetti, Sala dei Nove, Palazzo Pubblico, Siena, c 1339. Original painting, 1994, private collection, Barbara L. Legate, Nesbitt Coulter, London.

THREE SISTERS

1 & 2, inspired by two fragments of the fresco in the chapterhouse for Dominican monks, by Andrea di Buonaiuto [Andrea da Firenze], Santa Maria Novella, Florence, c 1365. 3, after a fragment of the fresco, "The Virtues of Good Government", by Ambrogio Lorenzetti, Sala dei Nove, Palazzo Pubblico, Siena, c 1339. Original paintings, 1995, private collection, Daniel R. Santola, Powers & Santola, Albany, New York.

IUSTICIA

After a fragment from the ceiling of the Stanza della Segnatura, by Raphael, in the Vatican, Rome, c 1510. Original painting, 1994, private collection, Powers & Santola, Albany, New York.

PORTIA

After an anonymous 19th century illustration. Original painting, 1994, private collection, Anne B. Gregory, Ottawa.

CONSCIENCE

After an anonymous woodcut from L'Iconologie Francoise, published in France, c 1766. Original painting, 1993, private collection, Michael & Gloria Neville, Ottawa.

NOTES ON THE TEXTS

Sources are given where possible.

All's love... Robert Browning.

MAAT
Lady of heaven... Sir E. A. Wallis Budge.

THEMIS
Soteira... Barbara G. Walker.

WISDOM & JUSTICE
Justice without wisdom... Froud.
Justice is the lawful... Aristotle.

THREE SISTERS
I sought my soul... Anonymous.
Seek the good... Sir Thomas Aquinas.
For there is no friend... Christina Rossetti.
She is a bowl... Virginia Woolf.
She is both... Elizabeth Fisher.
She stands between... Nancy Mitford.

IUSTICIA
Constant and perpetual... Emperor Justinian I.
Innate attributes... J.J. Bachofen.
The shield of... J. F. Smith.
The gladsome light... Sir Edward Coke.
Justice like the bright... J. F. Smith.

PORTIA
Quality of mercy... Shakespeare, Merchant of Venice.
Earthly power doth... Shakespeare, Merchant of Venice.
Mercy among the virtues... E. H. Chapin.

CONSCIENCE
A peace above... Shakespeare, Henry VIII.
That little spark... George Washington.
Even when there... Publilius Syrus.

Printed at the B.G.R. Studios Montreal.
Colour plates are on 24lb. laid finish Concerto paper.
The text is set in Palamino bold type
on 24lb. Antiqua parchment bond.

The full value
of your investment in this signed, numbered, collector's
album will be redeemed against
any purchase of an original painting
by the artist.